The Mobilepreneur's Manifesto: Conquer Business on the Go

Enahoro Imanatue

Published by Enahoro Imanatue, 2023.

THE MOBILEPRENEUR'S MANIFESTO: CONQUER BUSINESS ON THE GO

First edition. May 22, 2023.

Copyright © 2023 Enahoro Imanatue.

ISBN: 979-8223113331

Written by Enahoro Imanatue.

The Mobilepreneur's Manifesto

The Mobilepreneur's Manifesto

Conquer Business on the Go

Enahoro Imanatue

Chapter 1 Embracing The Online Environment

In today's digital age, the Internet has become an indispensable tool for businesses seeking to reach a wider audience and maximize their marketing efforts. However, harnessing the true potential of the Internet requires a solid understanding of its underlying technologies and the various elements that form its foundation.

As you embark on your marketing journey, it is crucial to familiarize yourself with the key pillars of online marketing: forums, websites, blogs, and email. These pillars serve as the building blocks of your marketing campaign, providing you with the means to connect with your target audience and promote your offers effectively.

While the Internet continues to evolve rapidly, staying updated with the latest technologies and trends that can enhance your marketing strategies is essential. New opportunities arise daily, presenting innovative ways to expand your reach and connect with potential customers.

In Chapter 5 of this book, you will discover how to integrate these various elements into a cohesive marketing system that operates around the clock. This system will serve as your reliable money-making engine, continuously attracting visitors from different corners of the Internet and converting them into loyal customers.

By understanding the intricacies of forums, websites, blogs, and email, you will gain the knowledge and skills necessary to leverage your full potential. Moreover, you will learn how to weave these elements together seamlessly, creating a robust network of marketing channels that work harmoniously to generate consistent revenue.

With your online presence established and your marketing system in place, you will be empowered to seize the countless opportunities the

Internet offers. Your business will thrive as you capitalize on the 24/7 nature of online marketing, allowing you to generate income even while you sleep.

Embrace the limitless possibilities of the Internet and embark on a journey to revolutionize your marketing efforts. Equip yourself with the knowledge and tools needed to navigate the online landscape successfully and unlock the true potential in the digital age.

Niche Sites

Carving out your space and establishing a solid online presence is essential in the vast Internet landscape, where countless websites compete for attention. This is where niche sites come into play – focused websites that target specific products or market segments, catering to the needs and interests of a particular audience.

Unlike websites that try to be everything to everyone, niche sites offer a unique advantage by honing in on a specific niche. Dedicating your website entirely to a particular enterprise creates a tailored and highly relevant online destination for your target customers.

The key to building successful niche sites lies in understanding your target audience and crafting an experience that resonates with them. This involves thorough research and analysis to identify your ideal customers' needs, desires, and pain points. By understanding their motivations and preferences, you can shape your niche site to meet their expectations and precisely deliver what they seek.

When developing your niche site, it's crucial to consider various elements to ensure its effectiveness. From captivating design and user-friendly navigation to compelling content and seamless functionality, every aspect of your site should be meticulously crafted to engage and convert visitors.

Furthermore, your niche site should serve as a valuable resource and authority in its respective niche. You establish credibility and build trust with your audience by providing high-quality content, relevant information, and expert insights. This fosters a strong connection between your brand and potential customers, increasing the likelihood of conversions and repeat business.

As you create niche sites, it's essential to maintain a strategic mindset. Continuously analyze market trends, monitor consumer behavior, and stay updated on industry developments. This will enable you to adapt your niche sites accordingly, ensuring their relevance and longevity in an ever-changing digital landscape.

Remember, niche sites are not just websites; they are powerful marketing assets that allow you to penetrate specific markets, drive targeted traffic, and generate higher conversion rates. By aligning your niche sites with the interests and preferences of your ideal customers, you position yourself as a trusted authority and attract individuals who are more likely to engage with your offerings.

In the vast online landscape, it's only natural to wonder if you have any control over the visitors who visit your website. Fortunately, the answer is a resounding yes, and the key lies in understanding the role of search engines in driving traffic.

When it comes to website traffic, search engines play a pivotal role. They are the primary gateway through which users discover new websites, products, and services. Among search engines, Google stands out as a dominant force, offering various resources and tools to help businesses generate targeted traffic.

You need to optimize your website's copy to leverage search engines effectively. By crafting compelling and relevant content that aligns with your niche, you can increase the likelihood of your website appearing as a search engine result when someone is looking for a specific product or service. This targeted approach ensures the right audience finds their way to your virtual doorstep.

The beauty of controlling the copy on your niche site is that it empowers you to attract a specific audience tailored to your offerings. By carefully selecting keywords, phrases, and relevant information, you can fine-tune your website to resonate with the needs and interests of your target market.

Google Keyword Tool

In the vast realm of online marketing, the importance of targeted keywords cannot be overstated. They are the building blocks of successful search engine optimization (SEO) strategies and are pivotal in driving traffic to your website. To help you navigate the complex world of keywords, Google offers a powerful and user-friendly tool called the Google Keyword Tool.

Accessible to anyone with an internet connection, the Google Keyword Tool provides valuable insights into keyword research. Whether you have a Google AdWords account or not, this tool empowers you to explore different worlds, uncover similar, high-paying keywords, and assess the level of competition associated with each keyword.

Imagine you're considering building a niche website centered around stamp collecting, a potentially lucrative venture. By inputting the keyword "stamp collecting" into the Google Keyword Tool, you can generate a list of related keywords that have the potential to attract traffic from individuals interested in collecting stamps. The tool provides information on advertising competition and approximate search volume for each keyword in the current month. Additionally, you can explore the estimated average cost-per-click (CPC) for keywords in a Google AdWords campaign.

Upon analyzing the results, you might discover that the search volume for "stamp collecting" is relatively low compared to other niches. For example, in June 2008, there were only 33,100 searches for "stamp collecting," which is relatively modest considering the vast number of Google users. Recognizing this, you shift your focus to another niche: scrapbooking. To your delight, the keyword "scrapbook" yields a significantly higher search volume, with 1,220,000 searches in June 2008.

As you delve deeper into the list of keywords, you'll notice that competition for some terms is fierce. To optimize your chances of success, your goal is to identify keywords with high search volume and low competition or with high CPC value. This meticulous research process enables you to compile a tailored list of keywords that align with your objectives. Remember, you can repeat this process with different words to discover hidden gems. For instance, you may also explore crafts-related keywords when targeting a scrapbooking site.

Armed with your carefully curated list of keywords, you're ready to create compelling copy for your website. By incorporating these keywords strategically, you can attract your target audience and improve your search engine rankings. Many marketers utilize blogs (web logs) to regularly publish fresh content, incorporating new keywords to expedite search engine indexing and drive traffic to their sales funnels.

Aim for a density of approximately 1 to 2% of the entire copy to ensure optimal keyword usage. It's essential to strike a balance and avoid keyword stuffing, as search engines like Google penalize sites that engage in such practices.

Suppose you need more time or inclination to write articles yourself; fear not! Platforms like www.upwork.com[1] provide access to talented writers who can create engaging content on your behalf. By purchasing sets of articles in bulk, you can maintain a consistent content schedule and ensure your website remains fresh and inviting. Additionally, signing up as a Google AdWords advertiser opens up the possibility of earning income by incorporating Google advertising into your site or blog.

---

1.   http://www.upwork.com

More About Blogs

Blogs can be a valuable and versatile tool when marketing your products or services online. While you can create a blog on a third-party site, hosting it on your website offers numerous advantages. By hosting a blog on your domain, you have greater control over the content and can seamlessly integrate Google advertising and affiliate marketing opportunities into your entries. This streamlined approach ensures visitors can easily land on your website without additional steps or hurdles.

If you already have a website and wish to incorporate a blog, platforms like Wordpress.org provide a convenient and accessible solution. These platforms allow you to effortlessly add a blog to your existing website, amplifying its functionality and engagement. Additionally, it's worth reaching out to your web host to explore any built-in options or tools they offer for incorporating a blog into your site.

A blog perfectly complements your sales offers, positioning itself as a source of valuable information. Search engines like Google recognize and favor sites with quality content, boosting your site's visibility in search results and attracting more organic traffic.

However, more than a blog is needed if it goes unnoticed. You must actively market your blog alongside your products or services to maximize its impact. One effective strategy is to make your blog easily bookmarkable on popular platforms like Technorati, Digg, StumbleUpon, and others. These platforms offer wider exposure and allow users to save and share their blog content easily. Additionally, leveraging relevant internet directories can further enhance your blog's visibility. Automating these processes ensures that your subscribers are promptly notified whenever you publish a new blog post while primary news feeds are simultaneously updated

Websites

When establishing your presence in the online world, your website plays a pivotal role. It can take various forms, from a simple sales page with email capture functionality to a more intricate membership site. The choice ultimately depends on your specific objectives and the nature of your target market. However, avoiding cramming all your offers onto a single website is crucial. Instead, aim to create multiple finely tuned sites to cater to the distinct audiences they attract. This approach enhances the effectiveness of your advertising efforts and enables you to build a robust network of related sites across the vast expanse of the internet.

While you have the flexibility to host your websites on a single hosting provider or multiple hosts, it's advisable to distribute your sites across different hosts. This precautionary measure ensures that even if one host experiences technical issues or a particular section of the internet experiences disruptions, your entire income stream won't be affected simultaneously. By diversifying your hosting arrangements, you can maintain a continuous online presence and ensure that at least some offers are always accessible to your audience.

When setting up your websites, simplicity is vital. Leveraging pre-designed templates and turn-key systems can significantly streamline the process. These resources allow you to establish your domain quickly, create persuasive sales pages, set up autoresponders to engage with potential customers, and even integrate payment collection systems. Today's technology makes it easier than ever to launch an online business. Rather than getting bogged down with complex scripts or endlessly tweaking the appearance of your site, focus on crafting compelling copy, utilizing existing templates, and implementing efficient systems. Embrace the power of automation and scalability, allowing your business to run smoothly and seamlessly. While occasionally seeking external assistance for specific features may be necessary, keep your technology stack simple, enabling rapid and efficient implementation as you expand your online empire.

Adopting a strategic website creation and management approach allows you to establish a solid online presence that resonates with your target audience. Multiple specialized sites, combined with streamlined technology and effective copywriting, will help you build a network of interconnected platforms that generate consistent traffic and revenue. Embrace simplicity, leverage available resources, and embark on the journey to establish your online empire with confidence and efficiency.

Forums

More complicated sites can include memberships and forums. You don't have to be a geek to set these up either. You can buy a forum that has already been developed by someone else through various sites for developers. They just transfer the domain to you and the hosting fees too and you can become the proud owner of a forum without ever doing a single line of code.

Forums have some pros and cons to them. You do have a captive audience where you can promote your products without being accused of spamming anyone. However, forums require more maintenance than a typical website because people do attempt to spam forums for their own agendas. So, you may be left either facilitating discussions or blocking certain users who abuse the forum rules. The payback is that you do end up having a direct connection to your customers and they are usually willing to buy from someone whom they trust.

One of the truly wonderful things about a forum is that you can bypass some troubles that you might get with email autoresponders. If you send large emails to your members often, the email provider can block you as a spammer. If you send instant messages on the forum to all your members, they can get your message right away and you aren't competing with anyone else's email or fighting their email provider for a right to land in their inbox. That doesn't mean, however, that you can't use email but that building a social network is becoming more the norm than mass email campaigns.

Email

Email remains a popular and effective marketing tool despite the emergence of new communication channels. However, it is crucial to approach email marketing cautiously and adhere to specific guidelines. Sending unsolicited mass emails, known as spam, can lead to severe consequences, including potential legal troubles. Obtaining explicit permission from recipients is essential to build a successful email marketing strategy.

On your website, it is imperative to provide visitors with a means to share their email addresses willingly. Implementing well-designed forms that capture not only email addresses but also physical addresses can be a valuable strategy. By offering enticing incentives or freebies in exchange for email sign-ups, you can initiate the process of funneling individuals into your community or sales pipeline. With explicit permission to contact them, your ability to effectively market to potential customers online will be unlimited. Therefore, prioritizing the acquisition of email addresses is a wise investment.

Creating an engaged email list allows you to establish a direct line of communication with your audience. It provides an opportunity to deliver valuable content, exclusive promotions, and personalized offers directly to their inboxes. However, balancing and avoiding overwhelming subscribers with excessive emails is essential. Respect their time and attention by maintaining a reasonable frequency of communication and ensuring that each message adds value.

Consider implementing segmentation strategies to maximize the impact of your email marketing efforts. Categorize your email list based on relevant demographics, interests, or purchase history. This allows you to tailor your messages to specific segments, giving subscribers a more personalized and targeted experience.

Furthermore, staying compliant with data protection regulations, such as the General Data Protection Regulation (GDPR), is crucial. Ensure that you have appropriate consent mechanisms, provide transparent data usage and privacy information, and offer easy opt-out options for subscribers who no longer wish to receive your emails. Respecting the privacy and preferences of your audience builds trust and fosters long-term relationships.

1

Chapter 2 Long Term Business Strategies

While it's essential to understand current strategies like Search Engine Optimization (SEO) and keyword research, it's crucial to recognize that the online landscape is ever-evolving. What works today may not guarantee success tomorrow, as search engine algorithms and platforms can change unexpectedly. Therefore, rather than focusing solely on short-term tactics, developing long-term business ideas that can withstand shifts in the digital landscape is wise.

To create a sustainable online presence, it is essential to diversify your marketing efforts and establish multiple channels for attracting and engaging customers. Relying solely on a single platform or technique leaves your business vulnerable to sudden changes or disruptions. By embracing a multi-faceted approach, you can mitigate risks and adapt to emerging trends or challenges in the online environment.

Target Hot Markets

When developing your market niche, it's crucial to prioritize the bottom line and avoid wasting time on stagnant or unprofitable markets. Instead, focus on identifying and targeting markets with existing demand and the potential for instant returns on investment. You can position yourself for immediate success and ongoing profitability by tapping into markets where desire exists.

To effectively capitalize on lucrative market niches, thorough research is vital. Stay abreast of the latest trends, consumer preferences, and market dynamics. Identify hot markets that are experiencing rapid growth and high demand. By aligning your offers with these thriving markets, you can position yourself as a solution provider for customers actively seeking products or services in those areas.

Create An Automated Sales System

1

Building an automated sales system that capitalizes on the strong desire of a target audience for a particular product or service involves following three straightforward steps. Implementing these steps allows you to streamline your sales process, capture leads, and maximize revenue generation.

Step 1: Develop an Irresistible Offer The first step in your automated sales system is to create a compelling offer that entices visitors to your website. This can be a free report, a discount coupon code, or any valuable resource that resonates with your target audience. The key is to provide an incentive that encourages visitors to provide their email addresses. This enables you to capture their information and initiate further communication.

Step 2: Craft an Engaging Sales Letter Once you have captured the visitor's email address, you can present them with a persuasive sales letter. This letter should deliver the promised free resource and showcase your products and services. Embed information about your offerings within the content of the report or email, strategically highlighting the value they provide. This lets you subtly guide prospects toward purchasing while providing valuable information and building trust.

Step 3: Incorporate Affiliate Offers Even if a prospect does not purchase directly from your product or service, you can still generate revenue through affiliate offers. Include information about relevant affiliate products or services that align with your target audience's interests. You can earn commissions on any resulting sales by recommending high-quality affiliate offers, providing an additional income stream.

To automate this sales process, it's crucial to set up an efficient email system. Utilize autoresponders to automatically deliver products, free reports, or any other digital assets to customers. This eliminates manual intervention and allows the system to handle the delivery process seamlessly. Additionally, configure your payment processor to integrate with your email autoresponder. This ensures customers receive their purchased products promptly without requiring continuous manual management of incoming and outgoing emails.

You can create an automated sales system that operates independently by setting up your website, offers, and autoresponders effectively. Once the system is in place, you can monitor the results and optimize your marketing efforts. The goal is to generate consistent revenue while minimizing the time and effort required to manage the sales process.

Create Self-Perpetuating Communities

So Harnessing the power of social networking can enable you to create vibrant and self-perpetuating communities that generate content and buzz for your products and services. Incorporating a forum or networking site into your online platform and initiating engagement with a few key individuals can create a snowball effect that propels community growth. While some may opt to incentivize participation by offering compensation to contributors, the decision ultimately rests with you. Alternatively, you can establish multiple user accounts and contribute under various names to foster the illusion of a larger community until more users join.

Forums and networking sites serve as valuable platforms for enlisting the efforts of others, effectively outsourcing content creation and promotion. Additionally, they offer lucrative opportunities to monetize through online advertising. By attracting a sizable and engaged user base, you can provide advertising space to external parties, generating revenue. Alternatively, if your primary focus is promoting your products, these communities offer a captive audience receptive to your advertisements and promotional content.

To foster the growth and sustainability of your self-perpetuating communities, consider implementing the following strategies:

1. Encourage Active Participation: Create an inviting environment that encourages users to contribute and engage with one another actively. Foster a sense of community by facilitating discussions, providing valuable resources, and recognizing and rewarding exceptional contributions.
2. Cultivate User-generated Content: Encourage users to generate and share content related to your niche. This could include product reviews, tutorials, success stories, or other relevant contributions. User-generated content enriches the

community and provides valuable social proof for your products or services.

3. Promote Community Interaction: Actively participate in discussions, respond to user queries, and foster meaningful connections within the community. Demonstrating your genuine interest and involvement fosters a sense of trust and loyalty among community members.

4. Leverage Influencers: Identify influential individuals within your target audience and collaborate with them to increase the visibility and reach of your community. Partnering with influencers can attract new users and enhance the credibility and reputation of your brand.

5. Gamify Engagement: Introduce gamification elements such as badges, rewards, and leaderboards to incentivize active participation and drive user engagement. Incorporating game-like elements makes the community experience more enjoyable and encourages continued interaction.

6. Continuously Evolve and Improve: Regularly analyze community feedback, monitor user behavior, and adapt your strategies accordingly. Stay updated with emerging trends and technologies to ensure your community remains relevant and appealing to users.

By implementing these strategies and fostering an environment of active participation, collaboration, and value creation, you can cultivate self-perpetuating communities that promote your products and services and become valuable assets in their own right.

Get As Many Affiliates As Possible

Attracting as many affiliates as possible is essential to maximize your affiliate sales and boost website traffic. One practical approach is to offer them a higher commission rate. While it may seem extravagant, providing fellows with 60% to 70% commissions can incentivize them to promote and sell your products actively. By delegating the selling process to an extensive network of affiliates, you can focus on creating new sites and developing additional income streams. Imagine having a team of 1000 affiliates selling your ebooks, allowing you to collect profits while expanding your online ventures. Conversely, with only a few companions, the returns may not justify the effort. Thus, it is crucial to maximize your income potential by leveraging the actions of a substantial affiliate base.

It's important to note that affiliates generate sales and drive traffic to your website. You benefit from increased exposure and potential customers by allowing others to publicize your offers. Over time, each site within your network gains value, and you may even consider selling the entire venture at a significant profit if you pursue other opportunities.

To effectively attract and retain affiliates, consider the following strategies:

1. Competitive Commission Rates: Offer attractive commission rates that motivate affiliates to prioritize your products over others. Higher commissions are a valuable incentive and make your affiliate program more appealing.
2. Clear Communication: Provide affiliates with guidelines, promotional materials, and product information to facilitate their marketing efforts. Establish a robust communication channel to address queries, provide updates, and offer ongoing support.

3. Performance-Based Incentives: Implement a tiered commission structure or introduce performance-based bonuses to reward affiliates who consistently achieve exceptional results. This approach encourages affiliates to surpass their targets and drives healthy competition within your network.

4. Training and Resources: Offer training resources, marketing materials, and access to exclusive content that affiliates can utilize to enhance their promotional activities. Providing valuable tools and knowledge equips affiliates to promote your products effectively.

5. Affiliate Contests and Rewards: Organize contests or reward programs recognizing top-performing affiliates. This fosters engagement, boosts motivation, and creates a sense of community within your affiliate network.

6. Timely Payments: Ensure prompt and reliable payment processing for your affiliates. Consistently meeting payment deadlines builds trust and encourages ongoing collaboration.

7. Performance Tracking and Reporting: Utilize robust affiliate tracking software to monitor affiliate performance, track sales, and provide detailed reports. Transparent reporting instills confidence in your affiliates and demonstrates your commitment to accountability.

Offer Free Items Frequently

While it may seem counterintuitive, offering free items is a powerful strategy for driving revenue on the internet. The key lies in leveraging the exposure and embedding your paying offers within these free items. By giving something away for free, you can tap into the viral nature of the internet and potentially generate substantial profits from the embedded links or offers within the free content. The goal is to create something that spreads rapidly across the internet, attracting significant traffic and potential customers. Even if you don't monetize the free item directly, having URLs or links back to your website within the content can result in a surge of website visitors and potential sales.

To encourage repeat visits and maintain audience engagement, consider offering free items regularly as part of the sign-up process. Many websites achieve this by providing a free monthly newsletter with valuable information and links to your offers. This approach allows you to continuously market your products or services while providing valuable content to your audience. Additionally, when readers find the newsletter helpful, they may even forward it to their friends, increasing your reach and potential customer base. For those who prefer physical newsletters, although the cost of mailing is higher, it can serve as a tangible reminder of your offerings.

Another effective strategy to generate interest and boost sales is to host contests for free items. This works particularly well on content sites with active forums. By encouraging users to contribute content in exchange for a chance to win one of your products as a prize, you not only engage and build your community but also create an opportunity to advertise your product throughout the contest. Even those who don't win the game will still know where to purchase your product, increasing the chances of future sales.

Remember, the goal is to balance offering valuable free content and strategically incorporating your marketing messages. By providing free items, whether it's through viral reports, newsletters, or contests, you can expand your reach, attract more customers, and ultimately drive sales for your paid offerings.

Monthly Subscriptions

Once you have successfully built a thriving community site, offering membership subscriptions can be lucrative. There are multiple reasons why implementing subscriptions is beneficial. Firstly, it creates a sense of exclusivity for the members, elevating their status above regular visitors. By granting this elite group access to additional discounts, special offers, insider tips, and exclusive content, you enhance their sense of belonging and make the membership appealing.

Secondly, monthly subscriptions provide a reliable source of residual income. Even a modest monthly subscription fee, such as $5, can accumulate over time, especially with enticing incentives like a $25 discount upon signing up. Many subscribers need to remember their memberships or find it inconvenient to cancel, resulting in recurring payments that continue for months or even years. This phenomenon is akin to unused gym memberships, where individuals hesitate to cancel in the hope of utilizing the service in the future. Some individuals may give up and forget about it altogether, making the process of unsubscribing challenging to find or navigate. If even a modest number of subscribers (e.g., 20) exhibit this behavior each week, you could effortlessly generate an additional income of $5,200 annually.

It is vital to balance the value of membership benefits and the subscription cost. You create a compelling proposition that justifies the recurring fee by providing unique advantages and exclusive content to members. Additionally, continually adding fresh and valuable content for members ensures their ongoing engagement and strengthens the perceived value of their subscriptions.

Remember, monthly subscriptions provide a reliable revenue stream and foster a stronger sense of community and loyalty among your members. By offering a range of enticing benefits, you can attract and retain subscribers while enjoying a passive income stream that continues to grow.

Good Ol' Marketing

In the ever-evolving landscape of the Internet, it's crucial to recognize that the strategies for success are familiar. They are, in fact, tried-and-true methods of making money adapted to the online business realm. Just because your business operates on the Internet doesn't mean that the fundamentals of good marketing no longer apply. They are even more relevant, and it's essential to remember that the key to selling your products and services lies in traditional advertising and creative offers.

While having a fantastic website is essential, it doesn't guarantee sales. Investing significant money in creating a feature-rich community site does not ensure success either. Even having an innovative concept destined to go viral can take time and effort. Why? Often, it can be attributed to a lack of good old-fashioned marketing common sense. This was the downfall of many dot-com companies that mistakenly believed that simply spending exorbitant sums on complex websites would yield substantial returns on investment. Unfortunately, they were mistaken, and investors in these ventures also suffered financial losses. Technology alone cannot replace the wisdom of effective marketing; instead, it should be utilized to enhance your marketing efforts. Avoid the same mistakes made during the dot-com bust and focus on simplicity while relying on timeless marketing strategies that withstand the test of time.

By prioritizing simplicity and leveraging classic marketing principles, you can confidently navigate the online landscape. Remember that while technology provides powerful tools, your marketing acumen will drive your success. By applying sound marketing strategies, you can effectively promote your products and services and achieve sustainable growth in the ever-changing online world.

Wash, Rinse, Repeat

When you discover a strategy or technique that proves successful for your online business, increasing your earnings becomes as simple as wash, rinse, and repeating. That's right. You can leverage the exact compelling offers and techniques and apply them across all the other websites you've created, each selling different product lines. You can ensure continuous success by duplicating your winning formula and diversifying your income streams.

By replicating the strategies that have yielded positive results, you can save time and effort while tapping into proven methods. Please apply the momentum you've built to new websites and product lines. This approach allows you to expand your reach, target different markets, and maximize your earning potential.

Remember, the key lies in adapting what works and tailoring it to fit your various ventures. You can achieve sustainable growth and create a robust online presence by consistently focusing on effective marketing techniques, quality offers, and customer satisfaction.

So, embrace the power of duplication and diversification to propel your business forward. You can amplify your earnings and build a thriving online empire by replicating your successful strategies across multiple websites and product lines.

.

1

Chapter 3-The Art Of Persuasion

As the Internet evolves, so does the sophistication of online buyers. What may have worked in the past no longer holds the same impact in today's marketplace, where visitors to your site have become discerning and selective. To successfully convert these potential customers, you must navigate their resistance and skepticism, leading them toward making a purchase. It would help if you mastered the art of seduction to turn your visitors into loyal customers.

The rise of social networking has also transformed the way business is conducted. It's intriguing that e-commerce, once considered daring and untrustworthy, has gained acceptance. People have become more comfortable with online payment systems but have grown cautious about the sellers they engage with. Building trust with potential buyers has become paramount before they commit to a purchase.

This is where the power of social networking comes into play. Buyers no longer have to rely solely on their instincts to determine trustworthiness. They can join online social communities and see what their friends are purchasing and what they have to say about it. To instill confidence in potential customers, many large companies incorporate feedback systems where buyers can share their experiences, allowing other visitors to assess the seller's credibility.

While obtaining the first sale may require more effort, the good news is that subsequent sales become significantly easier once trust has been established. Therefore, investing time in seducing your visitors and understanding the psychology of online sales seduction becomes worthwhile, as it ultimately boosts your bottom line.

Learn The Art Of Attraction

To seduce someone, you must uncover their desires and position yourself as the solution to fulfill those desires. However, this can be challenging as individuals often struggle to articulate their true passions and are more drawn to offers that resonate with them. Initially, take a broad approach to understand what makes your sales copy attractive or unappealing. Later, you can tailor your policy to specific demographic traits within your primary audience, further enhancing their inclination to purchase.

To begin, it's essential to identify behaviors that repel rather than attract. Avoiding these behaviors is a step in the right direction. Consider your own experiences in relationships and reflect on the most significant turn-off. It often occurs when someone becomes overly desperate to be with you, draining the energy from the interaction. People feel a sense of demand and depletion when someone defines themselves solely through their relationship with them.

The same principle applies to your sales copy. If your copy appears desperate to connect with visitors, it will repel them, leading to a need for more sales. While a "hard sell" approach may have worked in the past, the dynamics of the digital age have shifted. Internet users know that numerous options are available and won't settle for someone who lacks self-assurance.

Instead, the art of seduction calls for confidence. Your sales copy should focus on something other than convincing potential customers that you need them but should emphasize that they need you. Achieve this by writing authoritatively highlighting the benefits of a relationship with your products or services. Rather than pushing for a sale, educate customers, empowering them to make informed choices. Present a compelling case for why your offering is the best, rooted in your genuine belief. Maintain an upbeat and infectious tone that draws people towards you, encouraging them to approach you for sale rather than you pleading with them to buy.

Remember that throughout history, successful seducers didn't dominate their targets; instead, they presented irresistible offers. They understood that most individuals yearn to fulfill heartfelt desires and seek a trustworthy partner. By embodying this understanding and showing yourself as the solution, you can master the art of attraction and win over customers in the digital landscape.

Change Your Marketing Mindset

When crafting your sales copy, adopting a new mindset is crucial. Instead of convincing people to buy your product, focus on projecting confidence and positivity that captures their attention. Let this confidence shine through every word you write, from the captivating title hook to the comprehensive list of benefits. Your goal is to exude unwavering belief in the opportunity you're presenting to solve their problems, simplify their lives, help them make money, or fulfill any other targeted motivation within your core audience. It's not just about believing they will benefit from it; it's about knowing it with absolute certainty.

That's why aligning the products and services you sell with who you are as an individual is essential. This becomes even more crucial in social networking, as any dissonance between your online persona and your offerings can erode trust. To sell effectively on social networking platforms, authenticity is vital. The more your thoughts, feelings, words, and products align with your true self, the more confident you'll be in their value for yourself and others. If you're merely selling something for a quick profit, people will quickly discern your motives, and it can harm your reputation in the long run, even if you make short-term gains.

On the other hand, when you genuinely value what you're offering, others will sense your authenticity, fostering an aura of confidence and trustworthiness. By embracing this mindset shift and aligning your offerings with your true self, you'll enhance your marketing effectiveness and build lasting connections with your audience.

How Much Are You Worth?

In romantic relationships and life, your value isn't solely determined by your wealth, physical appearance, or age. You can attract an exceptional partner by simply being someone worth being around. With genuine confidence, even someone who may not fit societal beauty standards can attract remarkable individuals. When you believe in yourself and recognize your worth, it emanates a calm, soothing, and attractive confidence that draws others to you.

Individuals with high self-confidence tend to value themselves more than those with low self-esteem. This noticeable self-appreciation can create a feedback loop of admiration for you and your products, ultimately translating into substantial profits. You're not reading this ebook to learn how to close deals; you're seeking significant financial gains. So, how much are you worth? How do you value your products? Reflect on these questions when determining your pricing strategy. Are you aiming for viral growth by offering low-quality products, or are you valuing your time and expertise (such as through consulting)?

Your time and expertise are invaluable and should be priced higher than your products alone. Many people make a living by offering seminars and workshops, and there's no reason why you can't do the same online with today's technology. You can sell out far more seats online than you can at a physical venue. The more you value yourself and your offerings, the more likely this attitude will permeate your sales copy, magnetizing your offers and turning them into highly successful sellers.

Remember, your worth extends beyond monetary terms. Embrace your self-worth, recognize the value you bring, and let that confidence shine through in every aspect of your business.

2

How Much Is Your Customer Worth?

The attitude of appreciation and value begins with oneself, but it shouldn't end there. To successfully engage in the art of persuasion, your object of desire should be your customer. This doesn't mean you need to appear desperate for their attention; instead, it means that you genuinely appreciate and value their business and their relationship with you—regardless of its nature. Allowing room for the relationship to grow and evolve enables you to cultivate more profound and longer-lasting connections with your customers and products.

A simple act of gratitude can go a long way in strengthening customer relationships. Like waitresses who write "thank you" tend to receive better tips, expressing appreciation to your loyal customers can foster a sense of mutual respect and trust. It takes little time or effort to show your appreciation and offer them something that reinforces your bond.

By nurturing a relationship of appreciation and trust, you can create a positive and lasting impression on your customers. Recognize their value to your business, and let them know their support is genuinely appreciated. This approach can lead to stronger customer loyalty and increased satisfaction, benefiting both parties.

Simple Things To Remember

Whether in romance or business, seduction relies on understanding the psychology of desire. Similarly, successful online selling follows a similar path: indirectly approaching, building trust, and making a compelling offer. Here are some essential principles to remember:

1. Approach Indirectly: Avoid appearing overly direct or manipulative when engaging with potential customers. People don't appreciate feeling coerced, and overtly pushing your

agenda can create resistance that is hard to overcome. Instead, adopt a confident and genuine approach, showing interest in the visitor as an individual rather than simply a target. Maintaining a sense of authenticity increases your chances of progressing to the next step.

2. Occasional Unexpected Contact: Once you have captured someone's attention, it's crucial to maintain intermittent contact that is engaging, surprising, or helpful. These interactions should be short and manageable. This can be achieved through well-spaced email campaigns that offer valuable content. Gradually, the visitor will evaluate your trustworthiness and receptiveness to your messages.

3. Earn Their Trust: Trust is the cornerstone of any successful relationship, and it can be built indirectly through frequent contact or by leveraging mutual connections. For instance, promptly delivering a requested free report establishes credibility. Consistently meeting their needs without overtly selling reinforces trust and increases the likelihood of continued contact.

4. Make the Offer: Once trust has been established, it's time to present your offer creatively and irresistibly. By this stage, you should have a solid understanding of your target's desires and preferences, enabling you to craft an enticing proposition. Whether it's selling a report or promoting a week-long seminar, tailor your offer to their specific needs and aspirations.

By following these principles, you can navigate the art of persuasion ethically and effectively. Remember, it's important to approach potential customers with respect and authenticity, fostering trust and delivering value at every stage of the process.

2

Chapter 4-Connecting with Potential Customers And Crafting Compelling Stories

Storytelling has a remarkable power to captivate and enchant your audience. If you want to effectively communicate the value of your product and engage your visitors, harnessing the power of storytelling is essential. The story of the 1,001 Arabian Nights illustrates the persuasive force that stories can hold.

In this ancient tale, Scheherazade, the protagonist, is married to a king with a history of executing his wives. She proposes a unique strategy to save her life and protect other women in the kingdom. She tells the king a captivating story each night but intentionally leaves it unfinished, creating a cliffhanger. Intrigued, the king postpones her execution to hear the end of the story the next day. This pattern continues for 1,001 nights, and the king becomes deeply enthralled with Scheherazade's storytelling prowess. Eventually, he abandons his murderous intentions and allows her to live.

The power of storytelling lies in its ability to keep your audience engaged and returning for more. By crafting compelling narratives, you can establish a connection with your potential customers, captivating their attention and sparking their curiosity. Stories have a unique ability to evoke emotions, inspire imagination, and create memorable experiences. When done effectively, storytelling can foster a sense of loyalty and trust between you and your audience.

To connect with your potential customers through storytelling, consider the following strategies:

1. Know your audience: Understand your target audience's desires, needs, and aspirations. Tailor your stories to resonate with their interests and experiences.
2. Create relatable characters: Introduce characters in your stories that your audience can identify with or find intriguing. Develop their personalities and motivations to make them relatable and engaging.
3. Engage emotions: Incorporate emotional elements into your stories to evoke empathy, excitement, or anticipation. Make your audience feel invested in the outcome of the narrative.
4. Use vivid descriptions: Paint a vivid picture with your words, immersing your audience in the world of your story. Engage their senses and make the experience dazzling and memorable.
5. Maintain suspense and curiosity: Incorporate cliffhangers or unresolved elements that keep your audience wanting more. This builds anticipation and encourages repeat engagement.

The Elements Of A Good, Persuasive, Story

In the book "The Elements of Persuasion" by Maxwell and Dickman, five critical elements of a compelling story are discussed, each of which can impact the reader and leave a lasting impression profoundly. By incorporating these elements into your storytelling, you can influence the psyche of your audience and seamlessly guide them toward a desired outcome.

1. Passion: How you convey your story should reflect your genuine love and belief in its value. Instead of convincing your reader, approach your narrative with confidence and assurance.

Your enthusiasm will shine through your words and captivate the reader's attention.

2. Hero: Every compelling story features a protagonist, a hero, who embarks on a journey. Through their eyes, the reader becomes emotionally invested in the story, connecting with the hero and rooting for their eventual success. The hero serves as a relatable and engaging guide for the audience.

3. Antagonist: To propel the hero's journey, an obstacle or antagonist must stand in their way. This creates tension, risk, and the potential for failure. The antagonist adds depth to the story, highlighting the hero's strengths and weaknesses and intensifying the emotional stakes.

4. Moment of Awareness: The hero experiences a pivotal moment where they realize they have a choice and become aware of a greater destiny. This moment brings clarity to their journey and resolves any internal conflicts or paradoxes they may have faced. It represents a turning point and offers the hero an opportunity for growth and transformation.

5. Transformation: The successful struggle of the hero leads to change, either within themselves or in the world around them. This transformation results from their journey, bringing something new, extraordinary, and impactful. It is the ultimate resolution and the key to creating a powerful and memorable story.

By incorporating these elements into your storytelling, you can craft a persuasive narrative that resonates with your audience on a deep level. As your readers immerse themselves in your story, they will be influenced subconsciously, aligning their thoughts and actions with the journey you have presented. Ultimately, this alignment will help you guide them toward the desired outcome without realizing they are being sold.

2

Using The Five Elements In Your Sales Page

When crafting your sales page, you can effectively utilize the five elements of an excellent story to captivate your readers and compel them to buy your product or service. Let's explore how you can incorporate these elements into your sales page narrative, using the example of the Wall Street Journal's highly successful ad titled "Two Young Men."

1. Passion: Infuse your story with passion and conviction. Show your belief in the value of your product or service. The Wall Street Journal ad conveys the significance of being a loyal reader through the success disparity between the two protagonists. Your passion will shine through your words and resonate with your readers.

2. Hero: Introduce relatable protagonists whom your readers can connect with. In the Wall Street Journal ad, the two young men represent individuals seeking success after college. By presenting relatable characters, readers can see themselves in the story and become emotionally invested.

3. Antagonist: Introduce an obstacle or challenge that the hero must overcome. In this case, the difference in the protagonists' levels of success serves as the antagonist. Highlight the potential for failure or missed opportunities if the reader doesn't take action. Create a sense of urgency and demonstrate the risks of not utilizing your product or service.

4. Moment of Awareness: The pivotal moment occurs when the two protagonists' differences are revealed. It becomes clear that being a loyal reader of the Wall Street Journal led to one's transformation and extraordinary success. Help your readers experience their moment of awareness, where they realize the potential benefits and opportunities your product or service

can provide.

5. Transformation: Illustrate the change that can occur using your product or service. Show how it can take someone from an ordinary to an extraordinary life. Paint a vivid picture of the positive impact and results they can achieve. Encourage your readers to envision themselves experiencing this transformation and highlight the unique value proposition that sets your offering apart.

By incorporating these elements into your sales page, you create a compelling narrative that engages your readers and motivates them to take action. Use persuasive language, evoke emotion, and provide evidence of your product or service's benefits and outcomes. By aligning your sales page with the elements of a good story, you can effectively inspire your readers to imagine the transformation they can experience and ultimately decide to purchase your product or service.

2

Use The Power Of Imagination To Sell

The power of imagination is a formidable force that can be harnessed to sell your products or services. By tapping into your reader's imagination, you can go beyond mere description and inspire them to envision your offerings as the ultimate solution to their problems. People facing challenges often struggle to come up with solutions, and it is your role to guide them toward visualizing how your products or services can be the answer they seek.

A well-crafted story imparts a moral or insight. It sparks the reader's imagination, encouraging them to consider how they can resolve their problems by adopting the strategy presented in your sales letter. It is crucial to lead them gently, as individuals facing difficulties may have limited imaginative capacities. Your task is to inspire them to shift their focus from the problem to the solution—your product or service. Help them imagine how their lives will improve and highlight the immediate benefits they can expect by taking action now.

Suppose you have ever attended seminars promising rapid wealth or government grant opportunities. In that case, you may have noticed how they strive to inspire the audience by sharing stories of individuals who have used their products or services to transform their lives. By creating an atmosphere of excitement and hope, these seminars tap into people's emotions, driving them to invest significant sums of money in courses that promise to guide them on the path to success. Hope, a powerful motivator, lies at the heart of the hero's journey. If the hero gives up, the story ends. They must be inspired to push through the struggles and reach the moment of awareness that leads to a dramatic and transformative conclusion.

To effectively leverage the power of imagination in your sales strategy, consider the following:

1. Craft compelling stories: Create narratives that ignite the

reader's imagination and inspire them to envision their transformation through your product or service.

2. Lead with clarity: Guide your readers step-by-step, helping them see the connection between their problems and your offerings' potential solutions.

3. Highlight benefits: Clearly articulate the benefits and positive outcomes that await your customers once they take action. Paint a vivid picture of the improvements they can expect in their lives.

4. Appeal to emotions: Stir up positive emotions such as hope, excitement, and possibility. Create an emotional connection between your readers and the success stories of others who have used your offerings.

5. Provide evidence: Back up your claims with testimonials, case studies, or data that support the effectiveness of your product or service. Concrete evidence enhances the power of imagination by grounding it in reality.

Remember, by engaging your readers' imaginations, you can captivate their attention, drive desire, and motivate them to take the necessary action to purchase your products or services. Help them visualize a future where their problems are resolved and their lives are transformed. By painting this compelling vision, you can inspire them to embark on their hero's journey, ultimately leading to their success and your sales.

2

Drama And Controversy

Contrary to popular belief, your sales letter doesn't have to present a perfect, utopian vision of life if your reader buys your product. People are often more motivated by fear and curiosity than by an idealized fantasy. Engaging your readers' emotions through drama and controversy can trigger fear and hope, two powerful motivators that capture their attention and make your message memorable.

Like news agencies that thrive on powerful, dramatic stories from around the world or intriguing human interest stories, you can leverage drama and controversy to captivate your readers. These stories elicit strong positive and negative emotions, such as fear, repulsion, anger, or hope. By incorporating these powerful emotions into your sales page, you can leave a lasting impression on your readers' minds, far more than a Pollyanna-style story ever could.

When considering infusing drama or controversy into your sales page, it's essential to tread carefully. You want to avoid alienating or offending your primary audience. Aim for a level of debate that generates interest and discussion, especially if you have a member's site, but avoid crossing the line into causing hate or receiving threats. The goal is to build excitement and intrigue, not animosity.

Remember, every controversy in business presents an opportunity. When a company like eBay makes a controversial decision, such as disallowing info-product marketers from using their auctions unless the product is physically delivered, it sparks a firestorm of debate across the internet. Blogs endlessly discuss these controversial policies, and intelligent marketers seize the opportunity to sell products that help business owners navigate the transition from virtual to physical effects on eBay. These marketers capitalize on a controversy they didn't initiate, turning it into a profitable business venture.

Incorporating drama and controversy into your sales approach requires finesse and understanding your audience. By leveraging these elements effectively, you can capture your readers' attention, evoke powerful emotions, and drive engagement with your message. However, always be mindful of the line between captivating controversy and offensive content. Strive to ignite curiosity, spark discussion, and, ultimately, motivate your audience to take action.

The Story Of Your Sales Page

When creating your sales page, remember that it's still a sales pitch, albeit one told through a compelling story. After capturing your reader's attention with a hook, it's time to sell the benefits of your product or service. Your goal is to make it easy for them to envision themselves as the hero embarking on a journey that culminates in purchasing what you offer. Strive to be entertaining, educational, and dramatic while remaining mindful of being short-winded. Address potential customers' objections and provide the necessary information to overcome them.

The length of your sales page is subjective and should be determined by what is necessary to close the deal. There are differing opinions on this matter, with some advocating for longer, detailed pages while others prefer brevity and mystery. Experiment with both approaches and observe what resonates best with your audience.

You have already won half the battle once your reader engages in the story. Transitioning from account to offer may be noticed if done smoothly. Your readers will be so engrossed that they may attribute their discovery of your solution to their brilliance or good luck. They will be thoroughly seduced into action, whether signing up for a free report or purchasing. Determining the desired outcome for that particular sales page is up to you. If you have confidence in the exceptional nature of your offer, you can prompt immediate action by creating a sense of urgency. Encourage your potential buyers to act now to capitalize on this stroke of luck.

Avoid giving them time to think it over or explore competitor options. Infuse your sales letter with a sense of urgency that compels them to take action immediately while the offer is still available and beneficial to them. If you need help establishing a limited-time request, refer to Chapter 3 for suggestions and implement them at the end of your sales page.

By skillfully crafting your sales page story, incorporating persuasive elements, and instilling a sense of urgency, you can guide your readers toward taking the desired action and converting them into loyal customers.

3

Chapter 5-Crafting Irresistible Offers and Strategies For Success

The human mind is an extraordinary instrument that can be harnessed to work in your favor, even while you sleep. It operates much like a computer, diligently processing the information it receives. The saying, "garbage in, garbage out," holds here. However, instead of feeding your mind with unproductive content, you can plant seeds of creativity that will yield imaginative and captivating offers, propelling your business to new heights.

1. Cultivate a Creative Mindset: Embrace a mindset that fosters creativity. Open yourself up to new ideas, perspectives, and possibilities. Break free from conventional thinking and challenge yourself to explore innovative approaches. Allow your mind to wander, dream, and imagine without limitations. Nurture curiosity and embrace the notion that every problem has a solution waiting to be discovered.

2. Seek Inspiration: Find inspiration from diverse sources. Read books, articles, and blogs related to your industry and beyond. Attend conferences, workshops, and networking events to gain fresh insights and perspectives. Engage in conversations with people from different backgrounds and industries. Embrace the power of observation and learn from successful businesses and entrepreneurs.

3. Brainstorming and Idea Generation: Set aside dedicated time for brainstorming sessions. Encourage a free flow of ideas without judgment or self-censorship. Use techniques like mind mapping, word association, or random stimulus to generate innovative concepts. Collaborate with others and leverage collective intelligence to spark creativity. Remember that quantity breeds quality, so don't hesitate to create multiple

ideas.

4. Tailor Offers to Customer Needs: Understand your target audience deeply. Identify their pain points, desires, and aspirations. Craft offers that directly address these needs and provide tangible solutions. Please focus on your product or service's value and communicate it effectively. Consider bundling complementary offerings, providing bonuses, or offering exclusive discounts to enhance the appeal of your offer.

5. Experiment and Test: Be bold and try new approaches. Implement A/B testing to compare different offer variations and determine what resonates best with your audience. Monitor and analyze the results to refine and optimize your strategies. Embrace a continuous improvement mindset and adapt your offers based on customer feedback and market trends.

6. Create a Sense of Urgency: Incorporate scarcity or time-sensitivity elements into your offers. Limited-time discounts, exclusive bonuses for early adopters, or limited stock availability can create a sense of urgency and drive action. Communicate the benefits of acting quickly and highlight the potential consequences of delaying a purchase.

7. Provide Exceptional Customer Experience: Customer satisfaction is crucial for long-term success. Ensure your offers deliver on their promises and provide exceptional value. Build trust and credibility by delivering outstanding customer service and support. Encourage customer feedback and use it to refine your offers and enhance the overall experience.

By cultivating a creative mindset, seeking inspiration, brainstorming innovative ideas, tailoring offers to customer needs, experimenting, creating a sense of urgency, and delivering exceptional customer experiences, you can craft irresistible offers that captivate your audience and drive lasting success for your business. Embrace the power of creativity and let your imagination soar as you create offers that stand out from the competition and leave a lasting impression on your customers.

When No Means Yes

Harnessing the creative potential of your mind requires understanding the art of setting intentions. By establishing the right conditions and allowing your mind to work magic, you can generate innovative offer ideas seemingly out of thin air. However, one crucial aspect to remember is that your mind does not comprehend the word "no."

The word "no" is effectively ignored by your mind. This phenomenon occurs because your mind, like the universe, operates on positive language and intentions. It responds to the focus of your thoughts, regardless of whether they are positive or negative. Consequently, when you repeatedly tell yourself, "No more of this," your mind continues to generate more of what you are concentrating on, even if it involves negativity.

To illustrate this point, consider the typical example of being instructed not to think of pink elephants. Despite the explicit directive to avoid thinking about them, the intention is inadvertently set on pink elephants, leading to thoughts of them. This example showcases the power of positive choice over negative affirmations.

Now that you comprehend this fundamental aspect of your mind's workings, you can leverage this knowledge to create offers seemingly out of thin air. By positively aligning your thoughts and intentions, you can tap into your mind's natural ability to process and manifest your desired ideas.

Here's how you can put this concept into practice:

1. Set Clear and Positive Intentions: Formulate your intentions positively and precisely. Instead of focusing on what you don't

want, concentrate on what you want to achieve. Frame your thoughts and affirmations in a way that affirms your desired outcomes.

2. Cultivate a Creative Environment: Create a conducive environment for your mind to generate innovative ideas. Find a quiet, comfortable space to relax and free your mind from distractions. Engage in activities that inspire and stimulate your creativity, such as reading, listening to music, or spending time in nature.

3. Plant the Seed and Let Go: State your intention clearly and vividly in your mind. Visualize the desired outcome and immerse yourself in the positive emotions of achieving it. Once you have set your choice, release it to the universe and trust that your mind will work behind the scenes to bring forth creative offer ideas.

4. Engage in Other Activities: Focus on other tasks or activities after setting your intention. Allow your mind to work on the background's purpose while engaging in different pursuits. This detachment from the outcome allows your mind to process and generate ideas without conscious effort.

5. Stay Open and Receptive: Remain open to receiving insights and ideas that align with your intention. Be attentive to synchronicities, unexpected connections, or flashes of inspiration that may occur throughout your day. Embrace a mindset of curiosity and exploration, allowing new ideas to flow effortlessly into your awareness.

6.

By understanding that your mind operates on positive intentions and harnessing the power of this phenomenon, you can tap into your creative potential. Utilize the ability of your mind to process and manifest ideas, generating tempting offers that propel your business forward. Embrace the limitless possibilities when you positively align your thoughts and intentions, allowing your mind to bring forth innovative solutions and opportunities.

3

How Just 30 Minutes Of Time Can Produce Results

If Just as one push-up won't miraculously transform your body overnight, expecting instant results without investing time into your exercise routine is unrealistic. The same principle applies to your brain. However, the good news is that you can start experiencing results within 30 minutes of focused time.

A fascinating study on the brain's memory capacity sheds light on this concept. College students were given a task to think of as many words as possible that started with the letter "C" within a 30-minute timeframe. What researchers discovered was remarkable. Even after the experiment concluded, these students continued to generate new words for at least three days. Setting an intention and devoting just half an hour can profoundly impact the brain, signaling its significance and capturing its attention. Once the brain recognizes your commitment, it stores the information in a space where it continues to work on it, even after you shift your focus elsewhere.

Consider the implications of this insight. Imagine spending 30 minutes brainstorming different offers or marketing strategies to elevate your business, then moving on to other tasks. For the next three days, your mind will continue to generate ideas, tapping you on the shoulder at various moments to share its latest inspiration. Isn't it remarkable what 30 minutes of your time can yield?

By recognizing the power of concentrated intention within a limited timeframe, you can unlock the creative potential of your mind. Here's how to make the most of those precious 30 minutes:

1. Set a Clear Intention: Clearly define your intention before your dedicated 30-minute session. Be specific about what you want to accomplish, whether generating new marketing ideas, refining your business strategy, or crafting compelling offers.

2. Focus and Concentrate: During your 30-minute session, immerse yourself in the task. Eliminate distractions, create a conducive environment, and give your undivided attention to the objective you set. Engage your mind entirely, exploring different possibilities and allowing ideas to flow naturally.

3. Let Go and Shift Focus: Once the 30 minutes are up, let go of the task and shift your focus to other activities. Trust that your mind has absorbed the intention and will continue to work on it, even when you are not consciously thinking about it. Embrace the freedom to engage in different tasks, knowing that your mind is actively processing and generating ideas in the background.

4. Stay Open to Inspiration: Over the next three days, remain open and receptive to inspiration and insights. Pay attention to the subtle nudges and flashes of inspiration that arise unexpectedly. Keep a notepad or digital device handy to capture these ideas as they come, ensuring that they stay put.

Be Prepared At All Times

Picture this: You've dedicated your focused 30 minutes, allowing your mind to churn with creativity and innovation. Satisfied with your efforts, you decide to indulge in a relaxing shower. As the warm water cascades over you, you find yourself belting out the lyrics to the latest country song, lost in the moment. Suddenly, your brain taps you on the shoulder, eager to share another fantastic idea. You pause, startled, and exclaim, "Now? Wait, wait..."

Indeed, it often seems that the best ideas strike at the most inconvenient times—whether in the middle of the night or during our daily routines. But here's the crucial point: Be prepared. You've invested your valuable 30 minutes in unlocking the potential of your brain, and now it's critical to embrace and capture those ideas whenever and wherever they emerge.

Here's how to stay prepared and ensure that no brilliant idea goes unnoticed:

1. Embrace Spontaneity: Recognize that inspiration can strike at any moment, regardless of whether it's convenient or expected. Embrace the spontaneity of creative thoughts and welcome them with open arms.
2. Keep Tools Handy: Equip yourself with tools to capture ideas as they arise. Whether it's a small notebook, a digital device, or a voice recorder, ensure you have a convenient means of jotting down your insights promptly.
3. Create Idea Repositories: Establish designated physical or digital spaces to store and organize your ideas. This could be a notebook, a digital folder, or even a dedicated app. By having a central place to gather and revisit your thoughts, you can ensure they don't get lost in the chaos of everyday life.
4. Make Reviewing a Habit: Regularly review and revisit your idea repositories. Set aside dedicated time to browse your collection of ideas, allowing them to spark new connections and inspire further creativity. You never know when a seemingly unrelated idea from the past may hold the key to your current challenge.
5. Cultivate an Open Mind: Maintain a mindset of openness and receptivity. Remain curious about the world, actively seeking inspiration from various sources. Engage in activities stimulating your imagination, such as reading, exploring nature, attending events, or engaging in meaningful conversations.

Audio Recording Devices

When those brilliant ideas strike, it's essential to have a reliable method of capturing them for future use. Consider utilizing a compact microcassette audio recording device to store and preserve your valuable insights. These devices are designed to be highly portable, allowing you to carry them with you wherever inspiration may strike.

Using an audio recording device, you can effortlessly capture your thoughts in real-time, ensuring that no idea goes undocumented. Whether in the middle of a busy street, immersed in nature, or even taking a stroll, your trusty recording device will capture every spark of creativity.

Voice recognition software can be a game-changer for those who prefer to avoid transcribing their thoughts into written format later. With advanced options like Dragon Naturally Speaking or IBM's ViaVoice, you can effortlessly manage your brainstorms using speech-to-text technology. Speak into a microphone, and the software will convert your spoken words into written text, organizing and preserving your ideas for easy reference.

Imagine the convenience of being able to revisit your brainstorms at a later time without the need for manual transcription. Voice recognition software opens up new possibilities for efficient idea management, allowing you to focus on the creative process rather than getting caught up in the logistics of capturing your thoughts.

So, whether you opt for a trusty audio recording device or explore voice recognition software, you'll be equipped to preserve your ideas and inspirations effortlessly. Embrace the convenience and flexibility these tools offer, allowing your creativity to flow freely, knowing that your valuable insights are safely recorded for future use.

Journals Or Notebooks

When capturing those late-night epiphanies or flashes of inspiration, a trusty journal or notebook by your bedside can be your best friend. Keep one within arm's reach, ready to receive the gems that emerge from your subconscious mind after setting your intention. And don't worry—if you're on the move, you can still use this method safely, as long as you refrain from writing while driving. Have a small notepad available in your car to quickly jot down those brilliant ideas that surface during your journey.

A journal or notebook is an inexpensive yet effective way to record and track your ideas, especially when starting out. These tools provide a tangible and convenient medium for capturing your thoughts as they arise, ensuring no valuable insight slips through the cracks.

Make it a habit to regularly review and revisit your journal, allowing yourself to reconnect with past ideas and explore new connections. As you flip through its pages, you'll witness the evolution of your thoughts and ideas, and you may even stumble upon hidden gems that can be further developed and integrated into your business strategies.

So, whether you prefer the traditional charm of a physical journal or the convenience of a digital notebook, find a method that resonates with you and make it an essential part of your creative process. Embrace the power of pen and paper (or digital equivalents) to capture, preserve, and leverage the wealth of ideas that flow through your mind. Your journal or notebook will become a treasure trove of inspiration and a testament to your commitment to nurturing and harnessing your creative potential.

3

PDAs(Personal Digital Assistants)

Enter the world of Personal Digital Assistants (PDAs), the electronic counterparts to traditional notebooks. While they may come with a higher price tag than a simple pad of paper, many individuals swear by their functionality and efficiency. PDAs bridge the gap between capturing your thoughts and seamlessly transferring them to your computer for further exploration and organization.

With a PDA, you can effortlessly synchronize and upload your notes, eliminating the need for manual transcription. This digital convenience allows for easy access, searchability, and storage of your ideas. While PDAs may not offer the ability to sketch or draw, this limitation may concern only some, depending on their specific needs and preferences.

Investing in a PDA requires thoughtful consideration, as the cost can range from a few hundred dollars. However, the price may be justifiable if you find value in their advanced features, seamless integration with other digital devices, and the ability to have your ideas readily available in a digital format.

Choosing between a traditional paper notebook and a PDA ultimately boils down to personal preference and specific requirements. Some individuals thrive in the tactile experience of writing on paper, while others appreciate PDAs' digital versatility and connectivity. Consider your unique needs, workflow, and budget to determine which option aligns best with your creative process.

Remember, finding a method that empowers you to capture and preserve your ideas effectively is the goal. Whether you choose the simplicity of a paper journal or the technological prowess of a PDA, the key is to embrace a tool that enhances your creative flow and aids in transforming your thoughts into tangible actions and successful endeavors.

Send Yourself Reminders

Don't let those brilliant ideas slip away! By leveraging the technology at your fingertips, you can easily send yourself reminders through email or voicemail. Take advantage of your email program by composing a message to your email address, capturing the essence of your idea in writing. This way, you can later file it in a dedicated ideas folder, ensuring it's readily accessible when you need it.

Alternatively, if you can access voicemail, leave yourself a message with a concise and precise description of your idea. This way, you can listen to the recording later and transcribe the details into a more organized format.

One challenge with these solutions is that ideas often strike at unexpected times when you may not be near your computer or have your phone readily available. Consider carrying a small pocket notebook or a voice recording app on your smartphone to tackle this. These tools allow you to capture ideas on the go, ensuring no inspiration is lost.

The key is to find a system that works best for you and integrates seamlessly into your daily routine. Experiment with different methods and determine which approach aligns with your preferences and accessibility. Remember, the goal is to capture and preserve your ideas promptly so that they can be further developed and transformed into successful endeavors.

By embracing the power of self-reminders, you empower yourself to seize every moment of inspiration and harness the potential of your creative thoughts.

Be A Copy Cat

If you need help coming up with fresh ideas, why not look at what your competition is doing? By observing their successful strategies and tactics, you can gain valuable insights that can be applied to your business. Many entrepreneurs have achieved great success by emulating and adapting strategies that have proven effective for others.

Remember, imitation doesn't mean copying someone else's product or brand. It's about understanding the underlying principles and approaches contributing to their success and finding ways to incorporate those elements into your unique offerings. Just as Japanese goods evolved from being perceived as cheap knock-offs to being renowned for their exceptional quality, you can also refine and enhance existing ideas to create something even better.

However, exercising caution and avoiding infringing on intellectual property rights is crucial. Plagiarism and copyright infringement are serious offenses that can lead to legal consequences. If you have purchased resell rights or obtained product licenses, adhere to the terms and conditions specified in the agreement. These may include pricing restrictions, requirements to maintain original creator attribution or other stipulations. Respecting these terms safeguards both your reputation and your business's legal standing.

By drawing inspiration from others while maintaining integrity and originality, you can tap into a wealth of ideas and strategies that have already proven successful. Embrace the opportunity to learn from those who have paved the way and adapt their approaches to suit your unique vision and goals. Remember, innovation often arises from building upon existing foundations rather than starting from scratch.

Who To Copy

Focusing on successful marketers and networkers is essential when seeking inspiration and learning from others. You can easily find them by joining social networking sites, as mentioned in the resource section of this ebook. Look for individuals who have a large number of friends and actively promote their businesses through their profiles. By observing their strategies, you can gain valuable insights and apply them to your endeavors.

One common trait among these marketers is their adeptness at leveraging the power of the Internet to reach a broad audience. They utilize various platforms and techniques to spread the word about their offerings. For instance, they share their blog posts across multiple channels, use newsfeeds, and bookmark their content on platforms like digg.com and del.icio.us. While these actions may require additional time and effort, their increased exposure is well worth it.

Continuously monitor and learn from these successful individuals as they discover new tactics and applications for promotion. They often research for you, and you can adopt their strategies. Following them on social media lets you stay updated on their latest additions and evaluate if those approaches work for your business. Chances are, they will.

Another valuable source of inspiration is your competitors. Visit their websites, study their tactics, and emulate their successful practices. You can research online using search engines like Alexa to analyze your competitors' strategies. You can also identify websites that link to your competitors and target them to expand your network.

Explore your Internet survey by uncovering the keywords your competitors use in their campaigns. Incorporating these keywords into your website can improve your visibility and attract relevant traffic. Tools like the ones available at www.webceo.com[1] can help you analyze keywords effectively. If you prefer not to download an instrument, online website keyword analyzers are available by searching "keyword analyzer URL" on any search engine. Websites like www.submitexpress.com/analyzer[2] can provide beneficial results, albeit initially overwhelming, to enlighten your keyword research.

By studying and emulating successful marketers, networkers, and competitors, you can gain valuable insights, refine your strategies, and adapt proven approaches to your business. Remember always to show

---

1.   http://www.webceo.com/

2.   http://www.submitexpress.com/analyzer

appreciation for the ideas you borrow and approach emulation with respect and integrity.

Conclusion

Congratulations on reaching the end of "The Mobilepreneur's Manifesto: Conquer Business on the Go"! Throughout this book, we have delved into the exciting world of mobile entrepreneurship and explored the strategies, tools, and mindset required to thrive in the digital age. As you close this chapter, it's time to reflect on the valuable insights gained and prepare to embark on your mobilepreneurial journey.

In today's fast-paced and interconnected world, mobile technology has revolutionized how we conduct business. The rise of smartphones, tablets, and ubiquitous internet connectivity has created unprecedented opportunities for entrepreneurs to build and manage their businesses anywhere, anytime. The mobilepreneur lifestyle offers freedom, flexibility, and the ability to integrate work and life on your terms seamlessly.

Throughout this book, we've covered essential topics such as harnessing the power of mobile apps, leveraging social media for marketing and engagement, optimizing productivity on the go, and maintaining a healthy work-life balance. By embracing the principles and strategies outlined, you are equipped with the tools to establish a thriving mobile business.

Remember, at the core of mobilepreneurship lies the importance of adaptability and agility. Embrace technology and stay ahead by continuously exploring new mobile tools, trends, and strategies. As a mobilepreneur, your ability to pivot, innovate, and embrace change will be vital for long-term success.

Building strong relationships and networking with like-minded individuals is also crucial for mobilepreneurs. Seek out communities, attend conferences, and engage with peers who share your passion for mobile entrepreneurship. Collaboration and learning from others will expand your knowledge and open doors to new opportunities and partnerships.

Above all, always appreciate the power of a growth mindset. Embrace a lifelong learning approach, be open to feedback, and continually seek personal and professional development. As a mobilepreneur, your journey constantly evolves, and the willingness to adapt, learn, and grow will be instrumental in achieving your goals.

Now is the time to take action. Apply the insights, strategies, and tools this book shares to launch or expand your mobile business. Embrace the freedom and flexibility that mobilepreneurship offers, but remain disciplined and focused on your vision. Be patient with yourself, as success may not come overnight, but through consistent effort and determination, you will overcome obstacles and create the thriving business you envision.

Remember, the mobilepreneur lifestyle is not just about financial success; it's about creating a fulfilling and purpose-driven life. Strive for a healthy work-life balance, prioritize self-care, and celebrate achievements. As a mobilepreneur, you can design a life of freedom, passion, and fulfillment.

As you venture into mobilepreneurship, I

wish you every success and fulfillment. Embrace the power of mobility, harness the possibilities of technology, and let your entrepreneurial spirit soar. The world is at your fingertips, and you have everything you need to conquer business on the go. Here's to your remarkable mobilepreneurial journey!

3